W9-BIQ-874

SCHOLASTIC
News
Nonfiction Readers

Let's Visit a Dairy Farm

By Alyse Sweeney

Children's Press®
A Division of Scholastic Inc.
New York Toronto London Auckland Sydney
Mexico City New Delhi Hong Kong
Danbury, Connecticut

These content vocabulary word builders are for grades 1–2.
Subject Consultant: Dick Cates, Coordinator, Wisconsin School for
Beginning Dairy Farmers, Madison, Wisconsin

Reading Consultant: Cecilia Minden-Cupp, PhD, Former Director of the Language and Literacy Program
Harvard Graduate School of Education, Cambridge, Massachusetts

Photographs © 2007: age fotostock/Anton J. Geisser: 5 bottom right, 10; AP/Wide World Photos: 4 top,
17 (Bill Aldrich/Beatrice Daily Sun), 15 (Darron Cummings); Corbis Images: 1, 21 top (Fridmar Damm/
zefa), 11 (Thierry Prat/Sygma), 4 bottom left, 7 (Joel W. Rogers), 23 top, 23 bottom left (Royalty-Free);
Dembinsky Photo Assoc./Richard Hamilton Smith: 23 bottom right; Frank Lane Picture Agency: back
cover, 5 top right, 6 (Peter Dean), 4 bottom right, 13 (Wayne Hutchinson); Getty Images/Tim Flach: cover
JupiterImages/Reinhard/Premium Stock: 5 top left, 9; Nature Picture Library Ltd./Lynn M. Stone: 20
bottom; photolibrary.com/Lynn Stone/Index Stock Imagery: 2, 20 top; USDA Photo: 5 bottom left, 18,
19; Visuals Unlimited/Inga Spence: 21 bottom.

Book Design: Simonsays Design!
Book Production: The Design Lab

Library of Congress Cataloging-in-Publication Data
Sweeney, Alyse.
  Let's visit a dairy farm / by Alyse Sweeney.
    p. cm. — (Scholastic news nonfiction readers)
  Includes bibliographical references and index.
  ISBN-10: 0-531-16843-3
  ISBN-13: 978-0-531-16843-1
  1. Dairy farming—Juvenile literature. 2. Dairying—Juvenile
literature. 3. Dairy cattle—Juvenile literature. I. Title.
II. Series.
  SF239.5.S94 2007
  636.2'142—dc22   2006015658

2 3 4 5 6 7 8 9 10 R 16 15 14 13 12 11 10 09 08 07

CONTENTS

WORD HUNT

Look for these words as you read. They will be in **bold**.

bulk tank
(bulk taink)

dairy farmer
(**dare**-ee **farm**-er)

milking machine
(**milk**-ing **ma**-sheen)

calf
(kaf)

dairy cows
(**dare**-ee **cows**)

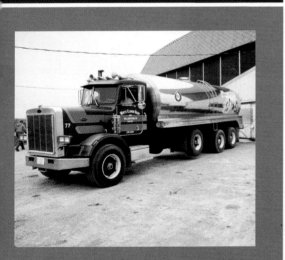

tank truck
(taink truk)

udder
(**ud**-er)

5

MOO, MOO, MILK!

These **dairy cows** eat all day. A **dairy farmer** knows that the more their cows eat, the more milk they make. That means more milk for people to buy at the store!

dairy cows

Dairy farmers make sure their cows have plenty of food.

A cow first makes milk when she has a **calf**. Milk is food for the baby cow.

The cow will keep making milk even after her calf is grown.

A mother's milk helps her calf grow healthy and strong.

Farmers milk their cows twice a day. Some farmers milk their cows by hand.

A cow's **udder** fills with milk. The farmer squeezes the bottom of the udder. Out comes the milk!

udder

This farmer squeezes her cow's milk into a bucket.

Today, most dairy farmers use a **milking machine**. The milking machine pulls milk from the udder.

Farmers can milk more cows at once when they use a machine.

This milking machine almost looks like a cow merry-go-round!

Where does the milk go when it leaves the cow's udder?

The warm milk moves through a hose.

Then, SPLASH! The milk falls into a glass jar.

The warm milk from the cow spills into this glass jar.

From the glass jar, the milk moves through a pipe to a **bulk tank**.

A bulk tank is like a huge refrigerator for milk. The milk stays cool here until it leaves the dairy farm.

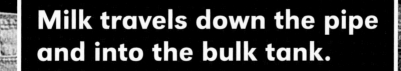

Milk travels down the pipe and into the bulk tank.

A **tank truck** takes the milk to a factory. Here, the milk is put into jugs and cartons. People later buy the milk in stores.

Thank you, dairy cows! Thank you, dairy farmers!

tank truck

A tank truck is cold inside to keep the milk fresh.

THERE ARE MANY DIFFERENT TYPES OF DAIRY COWS!

Brown Swiss got their name because they're brown and come from Switzerland.

Guernseys make milk that has a gold color.

Holsteins make more milk than any other dairy cow.

Jerseys are the smallest dairy cows. Their milk has the most fat.

YOUR NEW WORDS

bulk tank (bulk taink) where milk is stored and cooled on a dairy farm

calf (kaf) a young cow

dairy cows (**dare**-ee **cows**) cows that make milk

dairy farmer (**dare**-ee **farm**-er) a farmer who cares for and milks dairy cows

milking machine (**milk**-ing **ma**-sheen) a machine that milks dairy cows

tank truck (taink truk) a truck that brings milk from a dairy farm to a factory

udder (**ud**-er) the part of the cow that releases milk

WHAT OTHER ANIMALS GIVE US MILK?

camel

goat

llama

sheep

23

INDEX

FIND OUT MORE

Book:
Wolfman, Judy, and David Lorenz Winston (photographer). *Life on a Dairy Farm*. Minneapolis: Carolrhoda Books, 2004.

Website:
Moo Milk
http://www.moomilk.com/

MEET THE AUTHOR:

Alyse Sweeney is a freelance writer who has published more than twenty books and poems for children. Prior to becoming a freelance writer, she was a teacher, reading specialist, and Scholastic editor. Alyse lives in Las Vegas, Nevada, with her husband and two children.